Who Creates Laws?

US Government and Politics
Children's Government Books

Speedy Publishing LLC
40 E. Main St. #1156
Newark, DE 19711
www.speedypublishing.com

In this book, we're going to cover who creates laws and how bills are made into laws in the United States. Let's get right to it!

WHO CREATES LAWS AND HOW ARE THEY MADE?

The United States Congress is responsible for passing federal laws for the United States. There are two branches of Congress. One branch is called the US House of Representatives and the other branch is called the US Senate.

Here is a quick summary of the process:

A member of one of the two branches of Congress introduces an idea for a new law. He or she writes up the idea and sponsors it. Cosponsors consider adding their names to the new bill.

The bill goes to either of the two legislative branches depending on who proposed it. If a Senator proposed the bill, it will go to the Senate. If a Representative proposed the bill, it will go to the House of Representatives.

The bill next goes through a screening process by subcommittees and committees. During this process, it can be amended or changed.

enatów Europy
Meeting
the Association
ropean Senates
éunion
de l'Association
Sénats d'Europe

A summary report is put together to state the intent of the future law and whether it impacts other laws.

If the bill originated in the House, it will be voted on there first. If it passes by a majority vote, it will go to the Senate next. If it instead originated in the Senate, it will go to the House next. If both branches of the legislature approve it, it then goes to the President.

At this point, the President has the right to sign the bill into law or let it go into law without his signature. He can also veto it or pocket-veto it.

The House and the Senate must approve the bill and the President must not veto the bill before it is signed into law.

pages this ______ day of ________________, 20___,
to the undersigned authority that I sign and execute this
ingly (or willingly direct another to sign for me), that I
urposes expressed in it, and that I an 18 years of age o
undue influence.

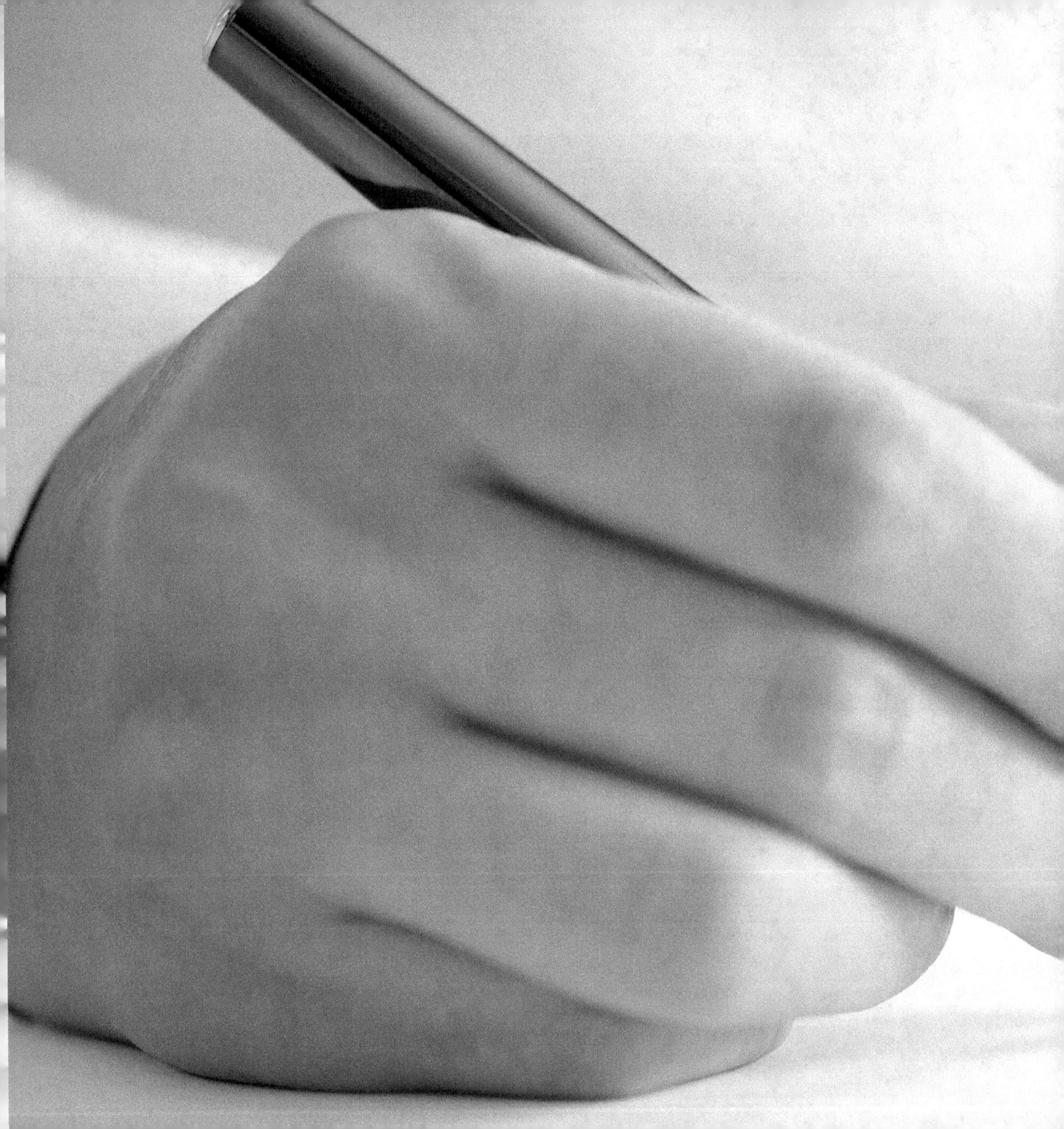

Now, let's look at this complicated process in more detail.

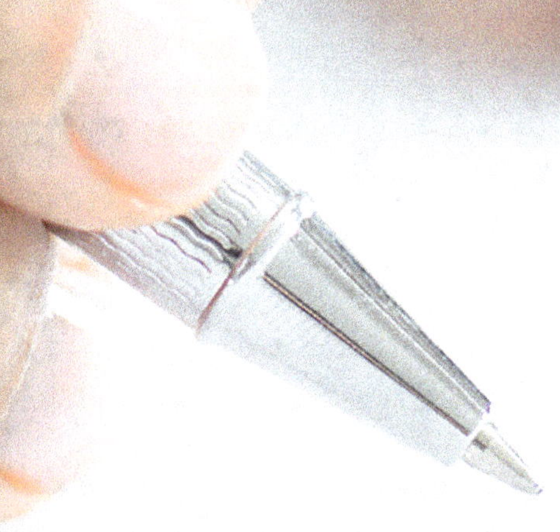

WHERE DO LAWS COME FROM?

Any citizen in the United States can propose an idea that eventually becomes a law. As an ordinary citizen you would have to propose your idea for a law to your local Representative. If your Representative thinks your idea has merit, he or she will begin the process of writing it into a bill. There's a lot of research involved in drafting a bill into a form that can be presented for a vote. Most ideas for laws come from Representatives in the United States House of Representatives or Senators in the United States Senate.

INTO THE HOPPER

In the House of Representatives, a proposed bill is placed in a designated box at the clerk's desk. This is where the phrase "into the hopper" comes from.

WHO SPONSORS A BILL?

Once a Representative or Senator introduces a bill to become a law, he or she is the bill's official sponsor. When the bill is placed in the hopper and is ready to be presented to the legislature, it is given a number and an abbreviation. The abbreviation H.R. means it was introduced by a Representative of the US House, and the abbreviation S. means it was introduced by a Senator from the US Senate. Once a Representative or Senator sponsors a bill, he or she rallies others to cosponsor the bill and add their signatures of agreement to it. Any member of the same body can help to cosponsor the bill. For example, if a Representative sponsored the bill, other Representatives can cosponsor it, but if a Senator sponsors a bill, other Senators will cosponsor it.

OFF TO A SUBCOMMITTEE OR COMMITTEE

The next step is the bill is handed over to a subcommittee or committee to be reviewed. For example, if the bill is about education, it would be reviewed by a subcommittee or committee that is involved primarily in education and creating laws for education. Sometimes, depending on the topic of the bill, it may be referred to several different types of committees.

THE COMMITTEE TAKES ACTION

Now it is time for the “mark up” part of a bill’s life. The chairman of the appropriate committee will determine whether the bill needs amendments. In most cases, the subcommittee will begin the process by holding a hearing.

cliftons
Senator Louise Pratt
cliftons

MR. BARRASSO
MR. WICKER

The bill can be amended or "marked up" at this meeting, but action can only be taken to move the bill through the process from the members of a full committee. The amendments to the bill must be discussed before they are adopted or not. The chairman then proposes that they take a vote to see if the bill can be moved favorably out of the committee. When the bill has been "reported out" of this amendment process, it is ready for the next stage.

THE COMMITTEE REPORT

At this stage, the chairman of the committee and his or her staff write a summary report about the bill that gives an explanation of why the bill is being proposed and the results of any hearings in the committees. If the bill has an impact on laws and programs that already exist, this information will be summarized in the report as well.

The statements from the majority of committee members will be included. If there are members of the committee who opposed the proposed bill, that will be stated in the report as well.

DEBATING THE BILL

If the bill originated in the House, the Speaker of the House will determine when the bill will be presented to the entire House of Representatives for debate, possible amendments, and final votes. If the bill originated in the Senate, the Senate Majority Leader will make that decision.

IN GOD WE TRUST

These two legislative branches have very different rules that determine how their debates must proceed. In the House, an amendment can only be suggested by a Representative, if he or she has received official permission. This permission needs to come from the Rules Committee. However, the Senate proceeds differently.

A Senator can suggest an amendment to the entire body without any warning or permission as long as the proposed amendment is relevant to the bill. A majority vote is required in either branch for amendments and also for final passage of the bill. Occasionally, amendments are moved forward by "voice vote." This type of vote is just made by the sound and volume of "yeas" for yes and "nays" for no.

REFERRAL TO THE OTHER CHAMBER

If a bill that originated in the House passes the majority vote, then it goes to the other chamber, which is the Senate, for debate and vote. If a bill that originated in the Senate passes with a majority vote, it's sent to the other chamber, which, in this case, is the House. Each chamber follows its own rules for debates and amendments. Either chamber can also approve the bill as it stands, table it, reject it, or make changes to it before passing it.

FINAL CONFERENCE ON A PROPOSED BILL

If the bill only undergoes small changes by the second chamber that reviews it, then it goes back to its originating chamber for a final concurring vote.

However, sometimes, by the time the House and Senate make changes to the bill, their versions are very different from each other so the bill doesn't read logically anymore. In this case, a conference committee is appointed to revise and reconcile these amendments. If the members of the conference committee can't agree on how the changes should be made, the bill dies there.

However, if an agreement is reached, the members submit a conference report that recommends the final changes to the bill. Both branches must approve this report, before the bill is passed. If either chamber doesn't approve the report, the bill dies there.

horized Signature
[Seal]

THE PRESIDENT'S SIGNATURE

Finally, the conference report about the new proposed bill has been sent to the President! If the President wants to approve this new legislation, he signs it and it then becomes part of the laws of the United States. If Congress is in session and the President doesn't sign the proposed bill within ten days, the bill will become law because the President didn't veto it.

If the President is strongly opposed to the bill for any reason, he can veto it, which simply means he will say it can't be made into a law. Also, if he takes no action on the bill after Congress has wrapped up its second session, he is essentially giving it a "pocket veto" and the bill dies.

OF, the parties have executed and sealed this Agreement
written.

By: ______________________

Authorized Signature

OVERRIDING THE PRESIDENT'S VETO

If Congress still wants the bill to pass after the President has not signed it into law, they can try to "override his veto." In order for this to happen, there has to be a two-thirds vote of approval in both the House and the Senate.

Awesome! Now you know how laws are created in the United States. You can find more Government books from Baby Professor by searching the website of your favorite book retailer.

Visit
BABY PROFESSOR
EDUCATION KIDS
www.BabyProfessorBooks.com
to download Free Baby Professor eBooks
and view our catalog of new and exciting
Children's Books

www.ingramcontent.com/pod-product-compliance
Lightning Source LLC
LaVergne TN
LVHW060508170826
845677LV00026B/1648

9798869432599